First Questions and Answers about **Weather**

Why Can't I See the Wind?

TIME
LIFE *for*
Children®

ALEXANDRIA, VIRGINIA

Contents

What makes the leaves fly?

The wind sends leaves drifting through the air.
It also makes kites fly and sailboats glide.
Sometimes the wind blows gently. At other times the
wind is so strong it blows the hat right off your head!

Why can't I see the wind?

The wind is made of moving air. We can't see air, but we know it is there. We feel it on our skin when the wind blows. We see how it makes smoke drift away from a chimney. And we hear it when it rustles the autumn leaves.

Did you know?
Air has tiny little bits of water hiding in it. This is called water vapor.

What are clouds made of?

Clouds are made of tiny drops of water. High in the sky, the air is very cool. This coolness changes the water vapor in the air into very small drops of water—or even into crystals of ice! These water drops or ice crystals float together as clouds.

Why does it rain?

It rains because the water drops in a cloud get too heavy to keep floating in the air. As the tiny drops of water inside a cloud bump into each other, they stick together and get bigger and heavier. When the drops are big enough, they fall as rain.

Did you know?
Tiny raindrops are small and round.
Bigger raindrops flatten out and are
oval-shaped as they fall.

Look out below!

What is fog?

Fog is a cloud that forms next to the ground. When warm air near the ground cools off, the water vapor in the air turns into tiny drops that we see as fog. Fog often appears late at night because the ground stays warm but the air cools off.

Hey! Watch where you're flying!

Did you know?
Fog can be so hard to see through that birds and bats get lost in it.

Why is it cooler at night?

Because the sun has gone down. All day long the sun shines down, warming the land. This makes the land heat the air near the ground. At night, this warm air rises up into the sky. The land cools off, and so does the air around you.

See you in the morning!

Where did the ice on my window come from?

That ice is called frost. When warm air outside cools off, the water in it forms tiny drops that stick to your window. Then, if the outside air gets very cold, those water droplets freeze and turn into frost. The frost makes beautiful patterns.

Help! I can't move!

Try it!
In the fall or spring, look for frost on leaves and grass early in the morning.

Why is it cold in the winter?

In winter, the sun stays low in the sky. The sunlight that reaches the earth is spread out. It does not do a very good job of warming the land. Winter days are short, too. The winter sun has little time to warm the earth.

Why can I see my breath on a cold day?

When you breathe in on a winter's day, the air is very cold. But your body warms it up and adds lots of water vapor. When you breathe out, your breath cools and the water vapor turns to droplets. Each breath you let out is like a little cloud of fog.

Did you know?
The same thing happens when water in a teakettle boils.
As the kettle whistles, water vapor rushes out. Once it's
outside the hot kettle, it cools. Then you see the water
droplets as steam.

21

What is snow?

Snow forms high in the clouds where it is very cold.
First, water drops freeze to make tiny crystals of ice.
Then more water drops stick to the crystals and freeze.
The crystals get bigger and bigger. When they are heavy,
they fall to the ground as snowflakes.

22

Did you know?

On very cold days, snow feels powdery. On warmer days, big, sticky flakes fall. The largest snowflakes are about as wide as a penny.

At last, I can fall back home!

What do snowflakes look like?

Snowflakes come in many beautiful shapes. Because of the way they freeze, snowflakes always have six sides. Some flakes are as flat as plates. Others are long tubes. Some even look like glass flowers.

Can you count my six sides?

Try it!
On a snowy day, put a piece of black paper in the freezer. When the paper is very cold, quickly take it outside. Let some snowflakes fall on it. Look at their shapes with a magnifying glass. What shapes do you see?

How are icicles made?

Icicles appear when dripping water freezes.
When warm sunlight shines on a snowy roof,
it melts the snow. Then water trickles down
the roof and drips off the side. In the cold air,
the water freezes to make an icicle. Each time
water drips down the icicle and freezes again,
the icicle gets fatter and longer.

Where does the snow go?

When the weather is warm, snow melts
and turns to water.

Some of the water turns into water vapor
and rises into the air.

Some melting snow flows into streams
and rivers. It helps fill up ponds, lakes,
and oceans.

Some water soaks into the ground.

Why does it get warm in the spring?

When the winter ends, the sun moves higher in the sky. The warm spring sunlight is not as spread out, so it feels stronger. Spring days are longer than winter days. The ground and the air have more time to warm up.

Do all clouds make rain?

No, they don't. Some clouds show that nice weather is here.
Others bring storms. You can learn to tell them apart.

High, white, wispy clouds often
come with good weather.

Some clouds are puffy, like giant balls of cotton.
They are usually a sign of nice weather.
But not always!

Low clouds that look like flat gray sheets
bring rain and drizzle.

One kind of puffy cloud is called a thunderhead. Instead of bright white it is a dark gray color. When a thunderhead comes, it brings rain, thunder, and lightning.

What is lightning?

Lightning is a giant spark of electricity. We often see it flash across the sky during big thunderstorms.

Inside a thunderhead, air rushes up and down. Bits of ice and water bump into each other. That makes electricity build up in different parts of the cloud. When there's too much of it, we see a FLASH! of lightning.

Did you know?
When you see a storm coming, you must go into a house or car and stay there. Don't stand under a tree— it's not safe!

Try it!
On a dry day, rub a comb on a wool scarf or sweater. Now touch the comb to a doorknob. Did you see it spark, just like lightning?

Why does thunder come after lightning?

Thunder is the noise that lightning makes. A flash of lightning heats the air around it. Then the air moves outward quickly, making the sound of thunder. We see lightning the instant it lights up the sky. But the sound of thunder moves more slowly through the air. So it always comes after we see the lightning.

Did you know?
Sometimes thunder sounds like a low, dull, rumbling noise. Other times it suddenly makes a loud *BOOM!*

What is hail?

Hailstones are balls of ice that fall during thunderstorms. Inside a cloud, air moves up and down. It carries drops of water up high where it is very cold. The drops freeze into bits of ice. When they start to fall, a little water sticks to them and freezes.

Sometimes the bits of ice keep going up and down on the streams of air. They get a bit bigger each time they freeze. Finally they fall as hail.

Hey! Watch it!

Did you know?
Hail usually falls in one place for only a few minutes.

When can I see a rainbow?

You can see a rainbow just as a storm is passing. These glowing colors appear when sunlight hits water drops that are still in the air.

Sunlight usually looks white, but it is really made of seven beautiful colors—red, orange, yellow, green, blue, indigo, and violet. When sunlight shines through a sky filled with raindrops, you can see all of the colors of light.

Wheeeee!

Try it!

Go outside with a parent on a sunny summer day. With the sun behind you, use a garden hose to spray water into the air in front of you. Make the spray like a fine mist. Can you see a rainbow in it?

How come my shoes get wet in the morning?

Hot days warm the ground. Then the ground warms the air above it. But everything cools off at night. Water vapor in the air turns back to drops of water, and the drops collect on the ground as dew. The dew makes your shoes wet when you walk on it.

Try it!
On a hot, sticky day fill a jar with ice water. Leave it outside for a minute or two. Now feel the outside of the jar. Can you guess where the water drops came from?

43

Why is summer so hot?

It's the season when the sun does the best job of warming the earth. The summer sun is high in the sky. Its strong rays shine down to heat the ground, the air, and us. In many places summer days are long, hot, and sunny. What a great time to be outside!

What will the weather be like tomorrow?

There is no way to know for sure, but you can listen to a weather report to get the best guess. The reports are put together by people who study the weather. These people use special tools to find out how warm and cold air moves. They also look at clouds. All of this helps them find out what the weather will be each day.

Red sky at night, Sailor's delight!

TIME-LIFE for CHILDREN ®

Managing Editor: Patricia Daniels
Editorial Directors: Jean Burke Crawford, Allan Fallow,
Karin Kinney, Sara Mark
Senior Art Director: Susan K. White
Editorial Coordinator: Marike van der Veen
Editorial Assistant: Mary M. Saxton
Production Manager: Marlene Zack
Senior Copyeditor: Colette Stockum
Supervisor of Quality Control: James King
Assistant Supervisor of Quality Control: Miriam Newton
Library: Louise D. Forstall, Anne Heising

Special Contributor: Barbara Klein
Researcher: Elizabeth Thompson
Writer: Andrew Gutelle

Designed by: **David Bennett Books Ltd.**

Series design: David Bennett
Book design: David Bennett
Art direction: David Bennett
Illustrated by: Anthony Lewis
Additional cover
illustrations by: Nick Baxter

First printing. Printed in U.S.A.
Published simultaneously in Canada.

Time Life Inc. is a wholly owned subsidiary of THE TIME INC. BOOK COMPANY.

TIME-LIFE is a trademark of Time Warner Inc. U.S.A.

For subscription information, call 1-800-621-7026.

School and library distribution by Time-Life Education, P.O. Box 85026, Richmond, VA 23285-5026.

Library of Congress Cataloging-in-Publication Data

Why can't I see the wind? : first questions and answers about weather.
p. cm. – (Time-Life library of first questions and answers)
ISBN 0-7835-0890-5. – ISBN 0-7835-0891-3 (lib. bdg.)
1. Weather–Miscellanea–Juvenile literature. 2. Meteorology–
Miscellanea–Juvenile literature. [1. Weather–Miscellanea.
2. Meteorology–Miscellanea. 3. Questions and answers.]
I. Time-Life for Children (Firm) II. Title: first questions and answers about weather.
III. Series: Library of first questions and answers.

QC981.3.W53 1994
551.5–dc20

94-16390
CIP
AC

Consultants

Ronald Gird is a meteorologist for the National Weather Service, National Oceanic
and Atmospheric Administration (NOAA).

Dr. Lewis P. Lipsitt, an internationally recognized specialist on childhood
development, was the 1990 recipient of the Nicholas Hobbs Award for science in the
service of children. He has served as the science director for the American
Psychological Association and is a professor of psychology and medical science at
Brown University, where he directed the Child Study Center from 1968 to 1993.

Dr. Judith A. Schickedanz, an authority on the education of preschool children,
is an associate professor of early childhood education at the Boston University School
of Education, where she also directs the Early Childhood Learning Laboratory. Her
published work includes *More Than the ABC's: Early Stages of Reading and Writing
Development* as well as several textbooks and many scholarly papers.